For Liz:

Let's stay together always.

For you & me:

May we have the courage
to discover the value of our voice.

Library of Congress Cataloging-in-Publication Data available.

ISBN: 978-1-7343928-3-8

www.thecultivatedgroup.co

Esmé the Curious Cat

the Curious Cat

Goes Global

Written By: EM Valentine

Illustrated By: Erin Spencer

Esmè jumped into the cockpit and started the engine
not knowing the answer, nor even the question.
With a curious heart she could hardly contain,
Esmè knew from her courage there was so much to gain.

Esmè found that from life she'd been charged with a task,
and that task was to follow wherever life asked.
With a plane full of fuel and her glasses in tact,
she began an adventure and tried not to look back.

As she began to fly higher, the higher she flew,
it amazed her the most that the world is so blue.
As she looked down below to the left and the right,
she could hardly believe the beauty in sight!

This climb up inspired her to take a deep dive.

It was in this moment she felt truly alive.

Her heart she looked into and let out a loud giggle.

She was so excited — she started to wiggle!

The world she once knew was now simply a sliver

of this great, great big world she now glimpsed a bigger picture.

She kept climbing and climbing, the world appearing much smaller,
with her laughter and wiggles the plane's balance began to falter.
The plane twisted and turned, spinning faster and faster.
She didn't quite know how she'd prevent a disaster!

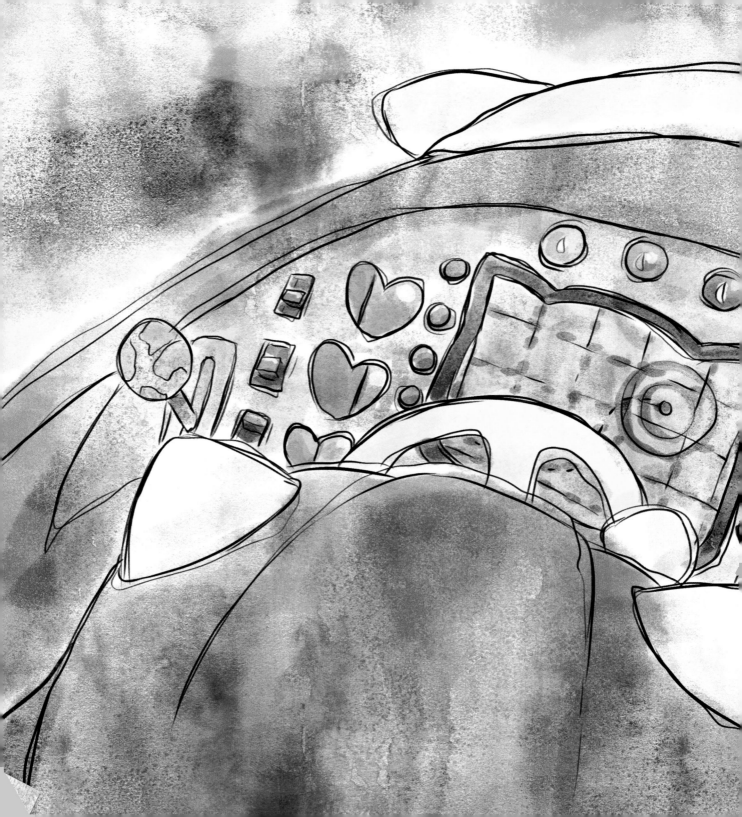

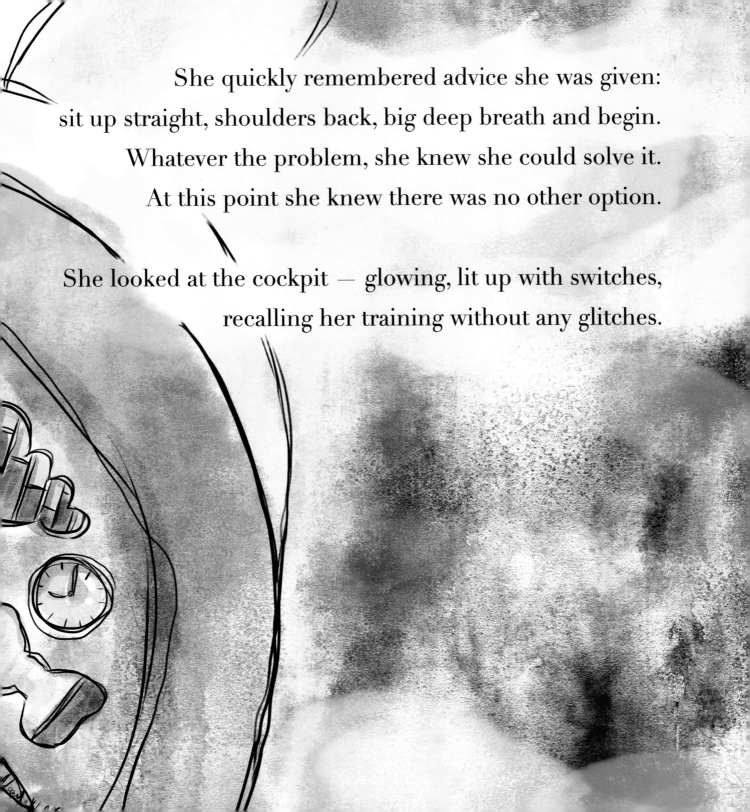

She quickly remembered advice she was given:
sit up straight, shoulders back, big deep breath and begin.
Whatever the problem, she knew she could solve it.
At this point she knew there was no other option.

She looked at the cockpit — glowing, lit up with switches,
recalling her training without any glitches.

She flipped — 1, 2, 3 — gained control of the aircraft,
did one flip for fun and was off with a laugh!
You see sometimes in life you'll be asked to be brave,
it's from truly these moments character you will pave.
These moments are fleeting, some big and some small,
you must choose to stand up, despite any fall.

Her true-north she trusts in — her heart knows the way,
passing London, Paris, Tokyo and even Bombay!
As she wanders the world with her trusty black glasses,
Esmè dreams of friends from all over — Canada to Damascus.
As our feline friend continued her initial ascent,
she pondered the air-time she already had spent.

Esmè hadn't quite realized of the world that she's seen,
how much her tastebuds craved a different cuisine.
Her stomach began rumbling and she started day-dreaming;
thoughts of pies, teas and cookies, even fruits made for creaming!

Food custom provides a different kind of connection,
she just couldn't wait for a world-wide selection.
Cuisine is how cultural custom prevails.
She dreamt of trying new dishes — cured meats, even snails!

The more she day-dreamed, the more she realized
how much being brave could wide-open her eyes.
Seeing the world with a light unfamiliar to most,
this privilege was one of which she would not boast.

Rather than bragging she planned to share it —
the experiences collected, lessons learned, cuisines tested.
She flew through the day, and into the dusk.
The stars began twinkling, twilight on the cusp.

Soon she realized it was time to be landing.
She peered out the side, searching for somewhere sandy.
A little nervous about the descension,
she knew sand would help with any tension.

As the plane quickly descended, gaining lots of momentum,
she knew she'd now need to have courage and then some.
With a quick 3, 2, 1 — the two wheels touched ground.
She looked right and left — no one else to be found.

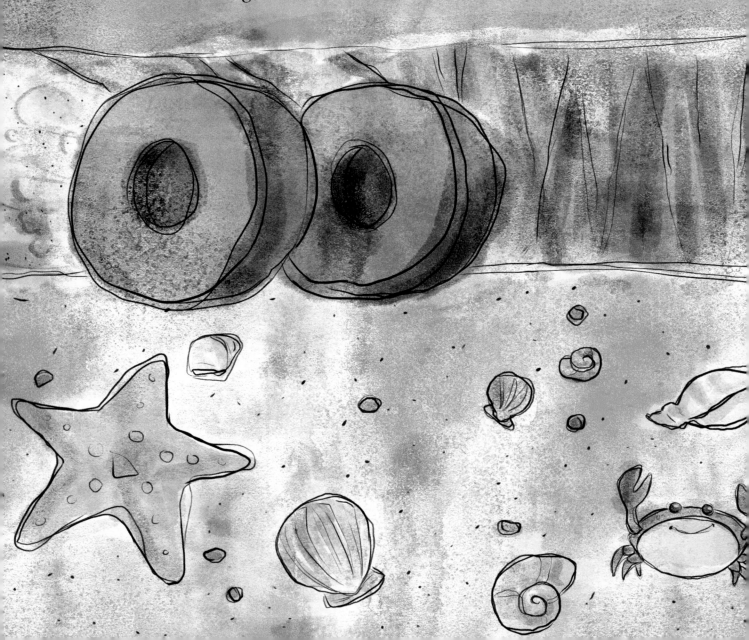

She unbuckled her seatbelt, jumped straight out of the plane
thinking just for a moment she just might be insane.
Her eyes wide with wonder, she blinked once and blinked twice,
cleaned her lenses — the prescription may now not suffice.
For out of the ocean appeared a huge figure,
two tons in sheer size — possibly even bigger!

Esmè became frightened — overwhelmed by the darkness,
only by moonlight did she see the figure's largeness.
She jumped back into the plane, overwhelmed by the night,
suddenly exhausted by seeming weeks of air-flight.

Pretending the figure was a great big dark blob,
her eyelids became heavy and head started to nod.
Into dream-world she drifted, mind wandering with ease,
feeling ever so slightly a faint Caribbean breeze.

As sleep took her over, eyes shut with one final thought;
although unsure where she was or what exactly she sought,
she knew she was grateful — and that meant a lot.
You see gratitude is the tool through which life truly takes place,
even when fearful, provides warmth — an embrace.

So embrace the adventure with all of your might,
rest your eyes, dear. Let your dreams be your sight.
Our story continues at the first signs of daylight…